One Day, Then Another

ONE DAY,
THEN ANOTHER

Poems by Kim Kwang-Kyu

Translated by Cho Young-Shil

WHITE PINE PRESS / BUFFALO, NEW YORK

White Pine Press
P.O. Box 236
Buffalo, New York 14201
www.whitepine.org

Publication of this book was made possible, in part, by grants from the Literature Translation Institute of Korea and Amazon.com and with public funds from the New York State Council on the Arts, a State Agency.

Cover photograph: "Seoul Street Vendor" by Dennis Maloney.

First Edition

Korean Voices Series, Volume 18

ISBN: 978-1-935210-54-2

Printed and bound in the United States of America.

Library of Congress Control Number: 2013947487

Contents

Part 3: The Power of a Forklift

Part 4: Foreigner, Limping

Part 5: Repose

FOREWORD

This is the tenth collection of my poems.

These works were written and shared with the public between summer 2007 and early 2011.

Add one to the last cardinal number in the decimal system, and the result is ten, which is the first two-digit number.

That being so, I reckon I've reached the point where I must start all over again.

So I quickly tie my old shoelaces.

—Kim Kwang-Kyu
Spring, 2011

Part 1.
Pureumi
(Pristine Beauty)

Remembrance of the Roots

Was it so dark and stifling
underground that these thick pine roots
could no longer endure and slowly thrust
their legs out of the earth? Did they abruptly
stiffen into a zigzag the moment they halted,
dazzled by the first glimpse of sun?
Or did the old pine simply forget
to call back to their underground abode
roots that had left their home?
Those pine roots, worn down
beneath the tread of hikers,
seem to be a brief remembrance
of the adolescent roots that finally
returned to their underground home,
unable to endure the frivolity above.

Pureumi (Pristine Beauty)

A fair and radiant forehead,
wide slit-eyes—
no plastic surgery on the lids.
A round, flat nose
no doctor has reshaped.
When she smiles, you see her teeth
haven't been straightened.
A few pimples on rosy cheeks.
Black tresses cover earlobes that,
unpierced, add an air of innocence.
Her legs aren't long like a model's.
Her stalwart figure gives forth
the body's fresh scent.
Simple attire.
Exuberant vitality.
Free of artifice
and gaudy makeup,
she emanates
young and vibrant beauty.
Hers is pristine youth.

Pine Grove in the Forest

There's not one straight pine
in the grove in the hillside forest behind the village.
No useful timber.
The trees slant slightly toward the east;
their branches stretch west and south
then spread toward the north,
shoot upward and sway, weighted
with winter snow, although their
blue-green needles are undamaged, alive.
These trunks, branches, and needles.
are nearly one hundred years old.
Neither vertical nor horizontal
but vagrantly straggling in their growth,
sometimes forking from the base
to spread like bushy pines,
Korean pines are a sight to behold
but they can't be pillars or rafters.
By virtue of this, they escaped being felled
and grew into this pine grove.
The sound of wind sweeping through
purifies listening ears
as the treetops high above
sway before my eyes.
There isn't one straight pine.
Picturesque as a folding screen,
the pine grove in the forest.
on the hill holds the full moon
then grandly floats it back to the sky.

Trumpet Vine

I hear
a guitar strumming
"Happy Birthday" somewhere
along the alleyway one July afternoon.
Something softly taps my head.
The outstretched, orange hand
of a trumpet vine creeping
up a jujube tree behind the fence
has turned to look at me.
It's like the innocent eye
of a child gazing at an adult.

Home by Myself

Standing on her hind legs,
front paws on the window frame,
Bokshil peers into the room and meets
my eyes. With no noise from inside,
she probably thought no one was home.
Buoyed by the coffee I had late in the afternoon,
I pore over writing I've long neglected
until, sensing someone's presence,
I turn and look outside.
There, high in the night sky,
the full moon peers into my window.
Everyone has gone.
I'm home by myself
but I'm not alone.

Grandmother's Hands

The Crab's Claw my grandmother tended so long
and left behind has quickly grown
knee-high in a white porcelain pot.
Beside the bed in a corner of our room
it still refreshes our eyes
and comforts our slumber with its exquisite scent.
More than a decade has gone by since she left
yet it's as though her warm hands are still near,
caring for her family day after day.

Sign of Autumn

Standing on the terrace stones
I was tying my old shoe
when, with a soft snap,
a hand brushed against my back.
It was the magnolia signaling autumn
as its silver leaves, lush all summer long,
have faded and now fall.

Eventide

After the tide ebbed
the barges spent a languid
afternoon sunk in the silt at the estuary.
Their long anchors cast ashore,
they rest like images in a still life
until white footprints of salt slowly emerge
as I dimly hear water rising and surging in
from the wake of the ferry on the distant sea.
Then reeds submerge,
waterfowl let loose their shrill cries
as the barges awaken and float.
A scented, red-tinged twilight pervades
when the waves flow in, awakening
wisps of memory strewn like seashells
as another day of my life ebbs away.

Autumn Butterfly

That evening when the lights and noise
from a makeshift stage in the public square
assaulted our ears and eyes,
the old poet I ran across on the lawn across from city hall
offered me his ice-cold hand.
Then, dragging a body almost too feeble to walk,
he receded slowly into the dark distance.
I remembered a book purchased five decades ago:
a collection of his poems, its covers tattered.
I wish I'd asked him to sign the book.
An autumn butterfly barely managed to fly away,
appearing about to drop and alight on the ground
like a leaf falling in the chill of a late autumn night.

A Native Squirrel

Two native squirrels
lived on Mt. Goeun.
They scrambled up stately pines,
nibbled pine cones, trundling them around
with their front paws, then came down
to the village below to help themselves to wasted food.
The plump one tried to leap from one branch to another,
fell, and was caught and eaten by a feral cat.
While taking a walk, I saw
the surviving squirrel.
Is it male or female?
Trapped on the mountain preserved like a small oasis
amidst Euju-ro, Morene-gil and Yunhhi-ro,
enclosed by high-rise apartments,
on that small mountain in the heart of the city
where it's so hard to come or go,
lives a solitary native squirrel

Maiden Spring

Autumn deepens, oaks
begin to drop their leaves.
The colder it gets, the more they hasten to disrobe
as if to cover the ground above their roots.
They thickly cover the earth
with their fallen leaves
but they suffer bitter cold,
naked in wind, rain, snow,
their myriad arms spread wide.
So saintly and beautiful,
the oaks resemble martyrs
as in the distance, maiden spring, yet unseen
approaches with small, careful steps.

Part 2.
Clothes on the Clothesline at That House

Clothes on the Clothesline at That House

Today as ever, no one seems to be home
in that run-down, tile-roofed house beside the road
down which I stroll.
Clothes of many colors
hang in the courtyard and on the roof,
sometimes swaying in the wind.
Stretched shirts, frayed pants,
faded skirts, little ones' panties,
large and small socks
guard the empty house.
Despite of the bright daylight, I can't see
where the household's head endures a hard day's work
or in what nursery school they've left the children,
but I can see that in the evening, a small family
lives together there.

Secret Voice, Recorded

Were we to hear once more
every word we've said thus far,
no pain would be greater.
With no excuses allowed,
we'd find it difficult to ever speak again.
Our very last words would be
simply, *I'm ashamed,*
or perhaps only a silence
no one could record.

Narrow Gate

The gate to enter into this world
is too narrow,
so we are born crying out
as though terrified by birth.
That day a light green bud sprang forth,
that time of verdant youth,
but the splendid moments all vanished like flames
and the darkening hours of future days,
ever more sad, draw near.
Ahead lies old age, pressed hard
along the edge of our growth ring.
Taking step after laborious step,
sometimes groping, crawling on hands
and knees, we approach that invisible realm
until we can barely manage
to slip out of this world's narrow gate.

At the Transit Station

When changing to train 2 at transit station 3
you must spend a good while going up and down
the steep steps in tunnels teeming
with passengers. But even amid the bustle
I spotted him. It's been half a century since I saw him.
His hair was gray, but I recognized his face
right away. We were each in a rush, so we briefly
clasped hands then parted. That
was it. We've never met again, although
we both live in Seoul day after day.

House at Mulmoe

I've returned, at last, to the house at Mulmoe.
Its stone wall of dry-stacked
black basalt is just as before. No matter
how fiercely the wind of Jaju Island howls,
that stonework never falls.
The many small holes
in those rocks make it strong.
Such is human fellowship.
Our pleasure and joy
each time we see one another
is full and solacing, like the sea.
Unending, like the tides, it returns.

Wine

I quit drinking at last
after a prolonged delay
to follow the clinic's prescription.
After quitting the beverage
I've been so fond of for the half a century,
a battle has begun
between the me who drinks
and the me who's on the wagon.
I'm torn
and can't take sides in this clash
between my selves:
the me who's been drinking for so long
is pitiable in illness and old age,
and the me who quit drinking
is cute as my grandchild at his tender age.
But it's quite likely that I'll break down,
my body and mind divided,
tormented, between these two.
I'm afraid it'll be much harder
to live well after that.

The Age of Silence

My grandchildren, who never knew silence,
are already in puberty
and have become reticent
with much innocent agony within.
It's hard to watch
them grope toward an unknown future
as they vigorously grow
while elderly gentlemen who lost their loves
long ago gather at the senior citizen center
to play cards, sing mambos, and mouth gibberish
at the top of their lungs the livelong day.
Youth and old age, just
half a life apart. It's disheartening
to hear them sing in their declining years,
while the silence of the homeless in the subway station
falls on no one's ears.

Room with a View

There's a beautiful two-story gabled house
beneath a lush green pine grove under a clear sky.
No one ever peeks out
of the window overlooking
the flowing river below.
I wondered if anyone lived there—
the house was too nice to leave vacant—
so flew like a dove, peered in the window
and saw such a mess.
A bundle of rags was on the floor.
Piles of dusty books,
old newspapers, a crushed noodle box,
a lidless kettle were flung about,
and left-over food was spilled everywhere.
And someone was asleep, snoring,
curled up like a homeless man.
I thought he was either a genius or an idiot,
yet Hölderlin might have been like him in his later years.

Older Sister Number Five

Born the last of three sons and four daughters,
I lost my mother early
and grew up among older sisters,
who were more like married women.
Now I've grown old, and some
of my brothers and sisters have gone to early graves.
One day, gazing at my old wife as she nagged me,
an old man resembling an overripe plum,
I suddenly recalled my second sister.
She used to make delicious kimchi,
was a good seamstress, a diligent housekeeper,
and she scolded her youngest brother the same way.
Growing older, I'm learning:
my wife has become like another older sister.

Shape of Stillness

Outside the windows, I see the blue-black
hillside of Mt. Baekryon,
its slope long and smooth against the sky.
Branches wave in the wind
as the warbling of cuckoos, orioles, doves
reaches the village.
A cool sylvan spirit
permeates me, as does the white wine,
and I can even see
how stillness looks
on a windless day.
When I'm by myself,
in the mountains or in a hospital room,
I see time in my rear view mirror, hiding
in the hills and valleys I often roamed.
How far I've wandered all these days....
Yet here I am again now,
just like this.

A Swarm of Flies

They rush onto
any open wound.
When shooed, they fly away,
then alight again on the seat of disease.
Those creatures torment us,
swarming over anything:
savory food,
a lion's inflamed eyes,
or a reeking trash heap.
Coexisting with an evil horde
we can't chase away, we learn,
little by little, to endure,
turn our eyes and look away.
Is this what wisdom, in the long run, is?

Homo Erectus

I glimpsed it through the flimsy curtain.
Encircling the pole with his front legs
and pushing himself up with his hind,
an ape was climbing the power pole.
His hands were white, his body black.
From where did he escape?
Amazed, I snatch the curtain open:
an electrician in black work clothes, white gloves
is climbing up to make repairs.
In my confusion, they looked so much alike.
Homo erectus shinnying up the pole.
The only difference is what's inside
the safety-helmeted head—
and the reaction when suddenly stroked.
In that moment, I wished to live a robust
life, fitting for a descendent of *Homo erectus.*

When the Fishmonger Arrives

As soon as the fishmonger shows up
in his small truck with loudspeaker blaring,
the whole village is astir. Over fences, through windows,
a seafood deluge exceeding eighty decibels invades every home.
Croakers, anglers, blue crabs, harvest fish, mussels,
stingrays, baby octopi, whatever, push their way in.
Five thousand *won* for six mackerel or flounder,
five thousand *won* for three pollock, hairtail, or dark hairtail,
five thousand *won* for four squids or squid from Sokcho,
two thousand *won* for one tuna,
two thousand *won* for five pike,
five thousand *won* for two octopi, live or dead,
four thousand *won* for two unsalted frozen pollock,
four thousand *won* for five salted or fresh mackerel,
four thousand *won* for a handful of marine algae,
ten thousand *won* for five king croakers...
As they flap their tails and bulge their gills,
the racket drills through our ears.
We don't mind the fishmonger calling out his list,
but we can't stand such cut rates,
so we cover our ears with both hands.
Suddenly the fish are carcasses again
and the truck disappears, spewing exhaust.
The noise from the loudspeaker dwindles away,
but the smell of fish spreads like an echo,
lingers with us no matter how much we wash—
just like the odor of our own slow deaths.

The Road Not Taken

It takes no more than fifteen minutes to walk from my house to University Y. I lived in Seoul with this big school nearby, but I went to University A, in the province of Kyungee.

I drove my sedan along the western highway and the west coast freeway nearly three hours—four in bad weather—commuting back and forth to work. As a poor driver, I always found the drive to be the biggest obstacle.

After ten years of that, I learned of a parallel route running along the Ahnyang River and detoured around the outskirts of Kwangmyung City whenever there was a traffic jam on my usual route. I was psychologically relieved to know we weren't just sitting at one spot, but this route wasn't any faster.

Perhaps I should consider myself lucky never to have been in a traffic accident during those thirty years of commutating.

Leafing through the newly edited *Encyclopedia of Road Traffic* one leisurely day, I spotted a turnoff running from the Cheolsan Grand Bridge southward to the western highway. Was this road recently developed, or was I just not aware of it?

If I'd known of this road, my commute might have greatly shortened since I could've taken the west coast freeway directly from the Ahnyang River instead of detouring around Kwangmyung City.

However, what's done is done and I can't change anything by worrying about it.

The same goes for everyone else, too.

Life moves along as unpredictably as traffic, fate out of one's control, there are paths you can't take, short cuts around traffic signals—so haven't I taken all that time, covered all that distance (many roundabout paths included), and ultimately ended up right here? Yet I still never know when and where I'll arrive....

Vacant House

Father passed on thirty long years ago;
mother spent the rest of her days in that house, alone.
A crumbling country house,
broken water jar under the jutting eaves.
A house you can't sell:
everyone has left for the cities.
Unhappy to leave it looking abandoned,
I had a new tin roof installed,
though no one lives there now.
Every year I receive a property tax notice
for this vacant property,
a house on its way out, flickering like a straw fire
in a corner of this aging orphan's heart,
this sinner who, against his will, has two homes.

Part 3.
The Power of a Forklift

Like a Petty Thief

Restlessly looking around like a petty thief
I hurriedly buried a box of ashes
under the regal cherry tree on the mountain slope.
I stealthily covered it with dirt and placed
on it a big stone.
Then I gulped some whiskey, took a moment
to have a few puffs,
ran down toward the village
as if chased, and quickly disappeared into the alleyway
leaving a plastic cup and a bag of chips
in front of the stone.
I wonder if anyone remembers seeing
that wretched son abandon his parent's ashes
so he could keep the cemetery fee for himself.

To a Teenage Mother

Sitting below the man-made waterfall near Hongjae Stream,
a girl in tight blue jeans and a baseball cap
is nursing
her newborn baby.
I see you could not escape
the torrential downpour, dear girl,
and got soaked through to your skin.
Dear girl, you've become the mother
of a pretty baby at an age when love is play
and no one chooses to have little ones.
Pity fills my heart
as I watch. You deserve a medal
from the Health Bureau advocating maternity.
Though wakeful during these sweltering-hot nights,
you'll harvest an early crop
from the seedling you planted while so young.
Mid-autumn will already be yours
before others' fearful winter comes.
Please have a fruitful summer;
raise a strong infant with your own milk.

The Power of a Forklift

Construction to replace an old drainpipe sets the whole village abuzz.
Its star is a huge forklift.
It drills a hole in the asphalt street,
pulls up a small drainpipe with a metal scoop,
then transports it to the dump truck.
It places the new drainpipe where the old
had been, levels it, dumps dirt
over it, and presses hard
with the metal scoop. Now
the last task is to pave the street again.
The forklift alone does all the hard work,
while five men assist with shovels and brooms.
The forklift earns fifty thousand *won* a day,
the workmen a daily wage of forty or fifty thousand *won*.
These men are the working poor.
Fees for supplies and removing waste are computed separately.
The management fee is handled in the usual way.

Division

Lest the tenants of a small apartment building
would have free access
to come and go,
the tenants of a towering luxury apartment building
blocked the passage
and put a chainlink fence across the road.
So it is with us.
Our nation was separated so long ago,
and we still live in a divided land.

Bear Hug

In childhood, long before I saw
a white polar bear
or a brown grizzly
in the zoo, bears
were my friends:
the teddy bear
I played with
and slept with in my arms,
panda bears wearing glasses,
cute moon bears
preserved on Mt. Jiri.
One brown bear
who ruled the animal kingdom,
devouring salmon
from rolling streams
and eating wild honey in the woods
quite suddenly turned and pounced.
It seemed he was about to fling
his paws around me and hug.
Before I could push his chest away,
he struck me with his curved front claw
and I dropped,
scapegoat of M&A.
Would I be able to rise again?
Could I come back to life?

Gazing upon Insubong

If the women carried away by the Qing
bathed themselves in the waters of Hongjae Stream
before crossing over Muahkjae
on their way back to Hanyang, their home,
no one was to speak of the shame of their defilement.
Is this not expedient for the nobility
who submitted to the foreign attack
and failed to protect their wives and daughters?
Thousands of women, children and commoners
were killed or disgraced when their ears were cut off
by Japanese soldiers during their invasion.
Where are the offspring
of the Choson people who still survive
after losing their country
at the twentieth century's dawn,
after having their mother tongue taken away,
their names forcibly changed,
their sweet daughters taken as prostitutes
during thirty-six years of Japanese occupation?
Oh, you who established so many committees
to right the wrongs of the past
but now squabble for rank and prestige!
Are you not ashamed each time you behold
the high and mighty Insubong?

I Don't Know Much About Human Geography

The Roman Empire at its zenith
encompassed most of Europe:
west from the Middle East
east from England,
south beyond the Mediterranean,
and north across the Alps all the way to
the Danube and Xanten on the border of the Netherlands.
Latin was taught in the Western world
as a required subject until the 20th century,
and Latin idioms are still often used,
just as Chinese characters are used in northern and eastern Asia.
Italian food and wine—
not to mention movies about the Mafia—
are loved by people everywhere in the world
as much as Chinese food.
Yet I've never heard descendents of the Roman Empire
claim their ancient sovereignty,
magnify their long-gone ancestors,
or senselessly falsify their history.
But I don't know much about human geography.

That Crying Baby

On the twelve hour flight
from Inchon Airport to Frankfurt,
a young white couple was traveling with
a baby with jet black hair,
and it endlessly whined and cried.
Though the tall dad held it and dandled
and the long-legged mom piggybacked and lulled
the baby stared around the entire time
and didn't stop crying.
Could it be hungry?
Could it be wet?
Nearby passengers made a few suggestions
but the baby still cried miserably,
save for a short time when it was put down on the floor
and allowed to crawl around.
Finally, the baby and new parents were gone
when our plane arrived in that far land.
That crying still rings in my ears,
those black, unforgettable eyes.
That little soul loath to leave home.

Press, Press, Tap, Tap

Dial the number on the phone, then you hear a cheery
melody and a woman's soft voice: Please press
the extension number of the department you need:
business department, 1
accounting department, 2
production department, 3....
So I began
to press hard as told
my registration number, secret code, and sundry other numbers.
Then she told me I had to begin again because
I had been too slow, so I began all over
and pressed all those numbers hard.
But again, she tells me I'm too slow....
When it comes to numbers, silence, patience and repetition
are of absolutely no use..
I can hardly follow
the automated machine's directions
with my slow hand
and clumsy finger . . .
Their fantastic service promptly blocks the connection
again and again.
This immaculate auto-reply system
turns every inquiry into numbers
but never once responds
if your slender finger just cannot press
nimbly and accurately.

Shameful Relationship

The local bus on the narrow road
is so crowded, it makes travel difficult.
The ladies' shopping bags are everywhere,
and youngsters rarely yield their seats
to the old and the feeble.
The young girl who kept her seat,
texting nonstop while
ignoring the old woman gripping a strap,
got off in front of the Star Hair Salon
and walked up the slope,
still making calls on her phone.
Why is she now ringing my doorbell?
I adjust my glasses and stare.
It's my own daughter,
her hair dyed blond,
in her brand new skintight pants.
We old folks who travel on the trolley or local bus
are none other than the dishonorable
parents of that child.

The Use of Poverty

No one ever knows
the names of the poor neighbors
who carried briquettes through the narrow sloped alleyway
of Shantytown and secretly brought rice and kimchi
to a widowed old man, and to a young girl
who was head of her household.
We do know, though
the name of the congressman who spoke for the poor
and received the Magsaysay Award for his relief work.
There was another highly honored man who proclaimed
the living conditions of the poor intolerable.
An advocate of the government, he knew
early in life that the poor outnumber the rich
or the middle class. He was a brilliant politician
who knew well how to use the plight of the poor.
Oh yes, a political animal will say anything
when hanging around with his pack.

A Corpse is Cold

A corpse is cold.
Even if a person dies young
you know by a single touch
that he's dead
but is not yet stone-stiff.
And it's surprisingly heavy.
It's surely the same form that once held
a life, whether short or long,
breathing in and out without pause.
Do you think you can take
the flesh and bones as your vowels and consonants,
nimbly tap on a keyboard
four consonants: c, r, p, s
two vowels: o, e
and juggle these lifeless letters
to easily create 'corpse,'
even play with them, like Legos?
You'll be a corpse some day, too,
so would you dare trample on a body which could,
indeed, be you, as if it's just the shadow
of someone else?
Dare you disgrace with your jangling loquacious voice
the body's final silence?
Dare you callously sever, destroy and burn
what is surely your own future?
You can't imagine your own corpse
but when you're a skeleton, here and now
will be, through your eyes, a distant previous life.

Insurgence

They attacked us like an occupation force,
brutally killing innocent citizens.
They set public buildings and private homes aflame,
plundered stores and temples,
then invoked martial law.
But they didn't last.
They fled, mere stragglers,
as another army of rebels claiming
to be liberators marched in.
They indulged in bloodshed, arson and plunder, too.
But they won't last long either.
Rumors are rife that a new
military group has been formed
under the banner of the National Self-Defense Force...
We've decided to sit silently on the fence.
We're not like any of them.

Part 4.
Foreigner, Limping

Southwest of Koryō

Rosewood left in a shipwreck underwater
for eight hundred years is now reborn as
sturdy agilawood. Tree, water and dirt,
silently melded over a long passage of time,
now rest beneath a celadon vase
on which apricot blossoms bloom,
clouds drift,
lotuses flower,
cranes dance.
I can almost catch lingering scents
of twelfth century Koryō wine,
hear echoes of a six-stringed harp
inside the vase's two-inch mouth.

Unfamiliar Country Station

For almost three hours
I've been on a local train,
stopping slowly at every station,
then moving slowly again.
We passed fields where
the farmland lies fallow,
crossed a bridge with no guard rails,
circled the foot of a mountain
on which many lizards, they say, make their homes,
before the train went through a tunnel and arrived
at an unfamiliar rural station.
A dilapidated church belfry perched
amid the snow-clad valley below.
Hardly any travelers get on or off the train here.
You can see a small Buddhist hermitage
nestled mid-slope on the mountain far away.
I'd like to spend the rest of my life there,
alone, sever all ties I've had for half a century:
no one would find me here.
Should I get off,
settle down?
While I hesitate, the whistle sounds
and the train begins to crawl.
Gazing back at that place, I see
it recede, farther and farther away,
now just another missed chance.

Old Temple

I didn't know
when I walked through the orchards on the hill
to the temple that the stone lantern, temple bell
and pagoda laid by the Silla people
in ancient days, were still there
in the serene stone courtyard.

I didn't know
that the stairwell Saint Uisang tread,
its stone steps steep and elevated,
has imaginary balustrades
on both precipitious sides.

I didn't know
that on the west side
of the Temple of the Great Amitābha,
is a boulder resembling Lady Seonmyo
which has been suspended
in midair for thirteen hundred years.

I didn't know
that I would go to the old temple time after time
and hearken to the wind chime there,
just as you'd listen to an old song.

I didn't know,
but when I walked out the colonnade
and down the slope, everything seemed
slightly changed.
Red fruit ripening, lovely,
in the apple orchard by the road.

Juniper

I guess you've been to Dohsan Institute.
Upon entering, you lower your head
as if bowing, walk over the raised threshold on the left,
peer at the floor of the Nongwoonjeongsa,
which was the dormitory during the Choson Dynasty,
go out past the Gate of Truth,
then walk up to the Mission Hall.
Have you ever noticed, on the right
along the way, over the front yard's outer wall,
a juniper stretching
and slightly atilt? They say this tree
whose needles are scarce and whose
maroon branches shoot every which way
is five hundred years old.
This homely juniper has lived
alone in the front yard on the right, or rather,
in the backyard of history, fragrantly enhancing
the institute's east side.

Blue Waters of the South Sea

Outside the windows, I gaze upon
the blue waters of the South Sea.
Sunlight glistens like fish scales
on the horizon where sky and sea meet.
Enormous freighters occasionally pass by.
The airborne sounds of waves and gulls
waft into the windows
of the lonesome room.
On days when the sea is tranquil,
I can see the color of eternity.
Sometimes, comfortably lying down
and gazing on the water
is better than medicine
for soothing pain.

One Dollar

A lake vast as the sea, its horizon far beyond.
Gliding over the dark water, a motorboat zooms by,
splitting the water wildly.
Ten tourists embark on a wooden fishing boat,
outfitted with an old car's steering wheel
and used now for private sightseeing.
Houseboats, clusters of reeds quickly recede
until the boat halts far out on the lake
while the guide explains the tour.
A small canoe hurriedly
approaches the pleasure boat.
Next to a woman, baby in one arm
and paddling with the other,
is a child with a huge snake around his neck
and his open palm thrust forth
One dollar, one dollar, he shouts.
They're a family of refugees.
Before the tourists can take any pictures,
the motor starts, raising wild waves
to chase the refugees' canoe away.
One dollar, one dollar....
The only common language
between the tourists
and the people in the canoe
*One dollar...*before the motorboat's noise
drowns it out.

Memento of Sicily

Gazing at Mt. Etna spouting opaque smoke
as if still unexhausted, we land
in the port of Naxos and climb the steep slope along the coast.
The Ionian sun changes color throughout the day.
A few Greek pillars remain
among the ruins of the ancient colosseum in Taormina.
I watch tourists from behind my sunglasses.
So many things attract my attention.
I just watch.
I take no pictures.
I just watch,
pausing a moment
instead of making tangible memories
until the short time remaining
means that we need to return.
This is what I remember of my trip to Sicily,
I don't have anything else.

Mediterranean Cruise

An American cruise ship leaving Venice
at dusk rings out
Louis Armstrong's song as if it's an anthem:
...What a wonderful world....
Excluding five things—
eating, drinking, sleeping, looking, shopping—
while sailing the splendid course
watching the sun set on the Mediterranean Sea,
everything else is the paraphernalia of a previous life.
My cell phone is turned off,
I don't watch the news
or read news magazines.
There's no agony
in this floating hotel
as we sail along gazing at land,
sky and sea.
You arrive at your destination unaware,
at the end of a comfortable journey
spent luxuriating in their pleasant services
while being shown the famous sites.
The simple beauty fades away but
your ID photo, resembling a cheap postcard
remains, and unreal images linger in your mind.

Floating Museum

A colossal ship with four towering
masts is moored alongside the dock.
Once used to sail back and forth to South America
the liner was built a century ago.
It stopped seafaring after half a century but still looks
just like new. A brightly lit lobby,
a restaurant with a view of the sea below,
bedrooms with neat and tidy closets and washstands,
a storage room with piles of goods and raw materials,
an engine room where stokers once burned coal,
and even a shed in a corner.
I hear they kept live cows, pigs, sheep and chickens
to be slaughtered for fresh meat,
for the meals to go with their wines.
I hear hens laid eggs even during the voyage,
lambs and piglets were born.
All the crew and passengers who occupied
the mobile village on the vessel have left this world
and the ship has become a museum
still afloat on the sea.
It rocks, every now and then, on the rolling waves.

Airport Near the Beach

A quiet airport near the beach.
A small jet leaves for Paris four times a day.
Its silver wings soar above the sea
in the bright Mediterranean sun,
through lavender-scented and crystal-clear air.
The staff closes the customs office at eleven a.m.
and steps out for lunch. A few foreigners
who missed their flights
have been lounging in the lobby
but now walk to the restaurant on the second floor
where they'll drink wine from Provence
while waiting for the afternoon plane.
They may remember this brief
unscheduled rest longer than they'll
remember some famed scenic sights.

Road to Eisenach

When I cross the low hillsides
in the region of Thuringia
where only a few cars travel,
I see expansive wheat fields below
and orchards sweeping around
the downhill side.
On the road to Eisenach,
past wide curves and sloping streets,
the rural landscape softly rises and falls
like a fugue for my listening ears.
In this fantasy, let me say,
the farmers working the fields
all bear a likeness to Bach.

Cavernous Pub, Esterházy

On a bleak wintry night in Vienna,
at a Christmas fair in the city's public square,
we try to warm ourselves with Glühwein,
but a damp bitter chill seeps in through our coats.
So we head for the underground pub in the sidestreet,
go down the steep subterranean stairs,
thrust the heavy entrance curtain aside
and step inside the cave. The underground hall
is abuzz with tipplers packed together like sheep.
Fluorescent lights dangle from the brick ceiling,
dimly illuminating the dark.
Many different tongues are making much noise
from every corner of the cigarette smoke-filled pub,
redolent with the odors of smoked ham, sauerkraut, wine.
Did all our forefathers live in caves?
Disregarding the main streets' elegant cafes,
they come to this cavernous, dark and dismal place
and stay until the wee hours of morning.
In the corner, we drain, by candlelight
three carafes of heurige, becoming, for once,
boisterous tourists, too.
Just more foreigners in Vienna.

Wine Display

When I have spare time in a store or supermarket
when in Europe, I loiter around the wine display.
Here it is, my favorite wine, St. Germain Bordeaux Supérieur.
It's 6.49 euros, which comes to about ten thousand *won*
For the quality, it's rather inexpensive. And look
at this, a 1999 Affentaler Spatburgunder, aged in oak .
German red will cost you nine point four nine euros,
and Chianti Classico seven point two.
Shiraz, which goes well with Korean food, isn't cheap:
A 2000 Durbanville Hills is priced at twelve,
and a 2002 Rosemount from Australia at twelve point six nine.
Chilean wines are competitively priced:.
a 2001 Santa Carolina (Reserva) is just six point nine nine.
I see they even sell eco-friendly wines.
Baden Weissburgunder for two point nine nine.
In choosing wine, you must discreetly select
what you like rather than selecting by price.
It's important that you sip and savor
rather than quaff it down,
but who has time to taste all these wines?
Life is so short and good wine so plentiful.

Niagara Falls

It takes ten hours and fifteen minutes by Air Canada from Incheon International Airport to Vancouver, where there are many scenic spots.

When traveling to Victoria, the capital of British Columbia, and near Calgary where the Winter Olympics were once held, you can regale yourself with the scenery of the northwestern American continent and the entire Canadian Rockies.

You still fly another four hours or so to Toronto or Buffalo, most often so you can see Niagara Falls.

These great cataracts cascading from Lake Erie toward Lake Ontario attract scores of tourists to the northeastern United States.

We're all abuzz as we take photographs in front of the powerful, deafening river, ride an excursion boat amid rainbows, clouds of spray, then watch this magnificent scene from the hotel's window across the way. I continually glance at the Falls—which send up spray through the night just as they did years ago—before turning, regretfully, around and flying for sixteen hours and forty minutes to get back home.

Oh well, I'm back after a nice, expansive trip. But I'm tired and dejected as I unpack: our entire nation is suffering from floods.

Still, people who don't spare time or expense, or who mind tedious long-distance flights, packing burdensome luggage, and getting dragged to all quarters of the world; and those who disregard their native land but visit countries far away, diligently looking out rather than in; and those who aren't content with our wide rivers silently rushing on and travel far for torrents and falls—no one calls these people adventurers, as in bygone days.

Foreigner, Limping

Everyone's a foreigner when abroad.
My left knee, injured two weeks
before this trip, hasn't healed.
Have I traveled too far?
Enduring the pain, I attended an international
conference, visited Schloss Molsdorf,
and saw replicas of ancient Greek sculptures
in a maze at the hall exhibiting stone monuments.
The left leg of Hermes was broken
and had only its iron core left.
It was just like this foreigner's left leg.
I'd limped all the way here only to behold
not West Germany's obliterated past
but my own future: I'm becoming ancient, too.

Part 5.
Repose

Repose

Life is a never-ending continuity
until we meet our death.
The heart ceaselessly throbs,
the lungs breathe.
Isn't love in our hearts
like that, too?
How sweet would it be
if our lives and loves could
take an occasional repose,
just as we rest on a bench
by the road when we
grow weary of walking.

The Day Darkness Beckoned

The voice on the phone
asked me to come to my publishers
office in the South Gate.
Much later, I realized the caller
was Mr. Chon. When I awoke at the crack
of dawn, I groped for my phone.
But he'd departed this world
long before the cell phone was invented....

That same day, a teacher who'd helped
me at graduate school telephoned.
He'd had an odd dream, he said,
and asked if I was doing all right.
Apparently, he'd heard a rumor
of my death. As a rule, no one
hears anything about anyone
when things are going well....

That night, stepping into the four-way crossing
after a meeting near Shinsu-dong, I tripped
on the base of a telephone pole
and fell. Afraid I might be seen,
I sprang up just in time to see the light
turn green and a cab dart headlong
out of the darkness.
What a narrow escape....

Debt Unpaid

I'm to blame for being lazy.
There was a chance I'd be stuck with them
after joining, so I just mailed
my fee and never attended their meetings.
But I did speak with their business manager
over the phone a few times.
He called to request my contribution or
to confirm my attendance at the next meeting.
I've heard his clear soft voice
but I never met him in person,
and now I hear that he unexpectedly
left this world.
Had I been to at least one meeting
and at least clasped his hand,
I wouldn't feel such regret.
Now he's gone,
and my debt to him unpaid.
Shame beyond words.
I'm to blame for being lazy.

One Day, Then Another

My best friends
in whom I'd confide anything, are
well acquainted with my ignoble deeds.
Now another of them has passed away.
Has some of my shame been covered
and thereby lessened?
No.
Now I have to keep to myself
what he knew of me,
so my shame is magnified.
Flowing in the veins of memory,
coming upon the retinas of closed eyes,
drumming, even in silence, through the ears,
ineffaceable shame multiplies
makes more annual rings
and leads me, I surmise,
to live one day, then another.

Mind at Stake

What a marvel this pulse of mine is,
still fluttering over sixty times a minute
from a fist-sized heart
which has been going pit-a-pat for seventy years
through hunger, fear, oppression,
during times of frustration, revolution, war.
But is this done by my own power?
I've lived, unceasingly breathing in and out
for seventy years, my two lungs adamantly enduring
cigarette smoke—which was like colonial opium—,
and shameful tuberculosis in a nation divided. But
is this, indeed, my own accomplishment?
When unwise thoughts arise, I gasp,
nearly suffocate. It gets harder and harder
to live, trapped in this narrow body
trusting heart and lungs
destined to cease one day,
I'd like to be released,
be freed from this heaviness. A mind
desiring to leave the body.
Whose is this white dream?

Elevator in a Dream

Alone in the elevator,
I pressed B4, remained
for some time
in that dark, six-sided space,
believing it would stop
at any moment
and the door slide open.
It never did.
I waited and waited
in vain.
I tried to press *Open*
but couldn't see in the dark.
I groped, but alas, no button.
It had faded into thin air.
How in the world!
I knocked and knocked
on the door, to no avail.
No cell phone.
Nothing to do but wait
to awaken from my dream,
dark as dark can be.

Old Photo Album

A photo of the two of us leaning against the rail
on a ferry sailing to an island far away.
Our hair blows in the southeasterly wind,
two faces surrounded by land and sea.
As the inlet fades away,
the island looms near.
I can't call him there,
nor send him an e-mail.
It's the face of a man
gone to the island where time ends.
We met for a single moment,
then were separated by the sea.
His life and mine
came together here then.
I snap those days open
then slam them shut again,
now that I can no longer evade
the gaze of his tranquil eyes.
He looks back at me
as though from the other side,
far beyond all memory.

In Memoriam: Mi-Baek

I didn't know I'd be reading a memorial poem
instead of wailing before you
whose eyes are now sealed in peace.
Oh, Mi-Baek,
are we not the friends who grew up
dreading flashlights bursting in on us
but dared write in Korean anyway,
casting all timidity aside?
We crept up the squeaking stairway
to the Haklim Teashop on the second floor,
across from the College of Liberal Arts & Sciences,
ordered a cup of coffee,
hung around all day
writing poems and reading novels.
The young men who listened to you read the first draft
of *Leaving the Hospital* as we sat around the coal stove in winter
are gathered here as elderly guests, offering condolences
to one another on this day as you leave.
Your voice was so calm
and your bearing so confident,
that we couldn't fathom
how you must've suffered
and persevered
to smile so tenderly.
Even before you heard your true love's voice,
you'd begun to write. A piece, then two,
three books, then four, to finally produce over the next forty years
a thick woodland of tremendous books.
Your mighty words found their way into the depths
of readers' souls, transplanted saplings of Korean literature
in the distant sod of Germany, America, France,
humbly and steadily.
Smoking cigarette after cigarette
in the dark outside the door of the Cathedral of Bad Honnef,

your heart was heavily burdened in your mother's last days,
yet you tirelessly told us stories
over wine through the night.
We remember your eyes, and the lips of a literary genius
unraveling a tangle of words.
You built a mansion spanning the world
while I fixed the weather-worn roof
of my old house in a corner of Seoul.
In page after page of manuscript,
you fashioned houses, hills, mountains, streams.
I think you're silently returning
to the home you once left in snow,
to the sylvan bosom where cicadas chirp;
you're winging, weightless, like a crane,
toward a newly built house by the sea
on the shore of Jinmok-lee.
Oh, Mi-Baek,
your future is now, sadly, gone,
but your warmth still lingers here.
Living on, we'll reflect on you
and never cease to reminisce about you
with our children and their children.

A Grave by the Sea

Midday in the muggy heat of 33° Celsius,
one hundred men of letters skipped lunch
to gather and mourn the deceased and dedicate,
with a glass of wine, two volumes of his complete works.
For him, we held an exorcizing dance
with an age-old musical narrative.
High on the hill behind the grave
stood a cowshed large as a factory.
Several cows eyed us; we smelled their manure.
On the sandy resort shore of Deukryang Bay,
they erected a great monument to Mi-Baek
and a towering pillar etched with his work.
A sea breeze wafted over the vast expanse of water
in front of his grave, as though caressing
his gently smiling soul.

Today, Eclipsed By Yesterday

I thought I heard a familiar voice,
turned around to see him waving at me.
I haven't seen you in a while.
I step forth and gladly clasp his hands,
but I can't get close.
He's stiff as a wax figure, and the distance
between us doesn't diminish.
A chasm brought about overnight.
Today, eclipsed by yesterday.
Though anxiously gazing at each other,
we can never again converse with human voice,
merely have a fleeting coexistence in ineffable space-time.
He stands like a rock in the river of memory.
Diving then sinking, alone, I drift along.
In this place, so repressive and stifling
though not a true nightmare, I ruefully
part with one I saw so many yesterdays.

The Last Perspective

All day long
magpies, doves,
locusts, evening cicadas,
long-horned grasshoppers, katydids, and crickets cried.
(They sang, we'll say in Western fashion
if that better suits your ear.)
Without their songs, how could we ever endure
midday's sultry hot-as-body-temperature heat?
Longing for cooler weather, we suffered through dog days.
How could we live through seasons,
so dry with little sun without love songs
sung so harmoniously by insects and birds.
All those thousands of hours
we suffered and endured
January's heavy, foot-deep snow
in the cold of fifteen below,
amid exhaust from twenty thousand cars
and noise from forty million cell phones.
Still, it's an age in which one dreads to die,
even after so many terrifying years.

Wet-Eyed

I didn't know in his lifetime
that after his departure
unstoppable tears would flow
from those small eyes;
that cries would spontaneously
burst out of mouths
once fouled with slanders, curses, shouts,
and now contorted with grief.
Thousands of people, unable to stay still
with eyes and mouths closed,
unable to pray alone,
quietly flocked near, lamenting as tears
gushed forth from deep down inside,
flooding all hearts beyond measure.
I believe these tears are the love
he so freely dispensed to everyone.

One's Dying Year

It was his final year.
His future came to a sudden end,
and he left his existence behind.
Time without end.... The rest
is granted to the living,
who continue inside empty parentheses,
unaware of the monotony therein.

NOTES ON THE POEMS

Page 17: Bokshil is the name of the poet's dog. Meaning Happy Dog, it is a typical dog name in Korea.

Page 18: A Crab's Claw (heliconia rostrata) is a tropical plant with floral bracts resembling a crab's claw. It is also known a False Bird of Paradise.

Page 22: Euju-ro, Morene-gil and Yunhhi-ro are streets in the heart of Seoul. Packed with highrise buildings and densely populated, they skirt the delta zone in which Mt. Goeun rises.

Page 31: Jaju Island is a volcanic island off the southeastern coast of South Korea.

Page 34: Friedrich Hölderlin (1770–1843) was a German poet. He spent the last several years of his life confined due to mental illness.

Page 35: Kimchi, a spicy national staple, consists of Korean cabbage and other assorted vegetables seasoned and fermented.

Page 36: Located in Seoul's suburban area, Mt. Baekryon attracts a good number of local sightseers and hikers year-round. Baekryon Temple on the slope adds serenity and beauty to the mountain. To the hikers' delight, at the end of their excursion, the octagonal pavilion atop the mountain offers a sweeping view of the nation's capital.

Page 39: A dollar was worth about 1063.5 won on January 7, 2013.

Page 49: A moon bear is an Asian black bear. Mt. Jiri, Korea's largest national park, is located in the Sobeck mountain range in southern South Korea.

M&A, or mergers and acquisitions, is part of the backdrop of the poem "Bear Hug," which is a term used in business for a hostile takeover.

Page 46: Hongjae Stream is a narrow river that meanders through Seoul and merges with the lower Han River.

Page 50: Qing - The last imperial dynasty of China, ruling from 1644 to 1912, they invaded Korea in both 1627 and 1636. Japan annexed Korea in 1910 and occuied it until the end of World War II.

The term "Choson People" refers to Koreans. It began to be used during the Japanese occupation of Korea and has been widely used ever since.

Insubong is one of the three summits of Mount Bukhan in Seoul.

Page 51: Xanten is a historic town in the North Rhine-Westphalia state of Germany.

Page 55: The Magsaysay Award is given annually by the Ramon Magsaysay Award Foundation to honor the late president of the Phillipines and to perpetuate his example of integrity in public service and pragmatic idealism within a democratic society.

Page 57: This poem alludes to the universal pattern in which a political power surges into a society and collides against the existing regime, ultimately bringing havoc on the components of the society who usually find themselves unable to resist much. Here, the abstract picture delineates no particular historical upheaval but depicts a striking instance of human destruction by human forces.

Page 61: Koryō was an ancient Korean dynasty that originated in A.D. 918 and lasted until 1392.

Page 63: This poem refers to Buseoksa (Floating Rock) Temple.

Silla was one of the ancient Three Kingdoms of Korea. Established as a nation in B.C. 57, it saw its demise in A.D. 935.

Born in A.D. 625, Saint Uisang was a great Buddhist monk who taught the way to Nirvana to his disciples and the people of his era. He died in 702, leaving behind him a legacy of great teachings and an exemplary life.

Saint Uisang founded the Buseoksa Temple in Yeongju in 676. In the vicinity of the temple stands Muryangsujeon, the oldest wooden building of the era and a national treasure. Muryangsujeon houses a great statue of Amitābha (Buddha).

Uisang met Lady Seonmyo in Dang, China while he was studying.

Uisang told Seonmyo that he was going back to his country, and Seonmyo jumped into the sea and drowned herself after realizing that Uisang's boat had left for Korea. After her death, Seonmyo became a dragon and followed Uisang to Korea to protect and be with him. When Uisang ran into difficulty in building the new temple, and they tried to stop him, Uisang brought down three stones from heaven to stop the crowd that had gathered to block him. One of the stones that floated down from the heavens resembles a dragon and now stands to the left of the main hall, Muryangsujeon. The temple is named after this "floating rock" story.

Page 64: Dohsan Institute was built in 1574 in the town of Dohsan to extol and spread the great virtues and teachings of Lee Whang, a vassal and scholar of Sung Confucianism during the Choson Dynasty.

The Choson Dynasty ruled over the Korean Peninsula and the surrounding islands from 1392 to 1897.

Page 67: Taormina is a small city located on the northern extremity of Mt. Etna in eastern Sicily. The city is well-known for its history dating back to the time before Christ and for its beautiful view of the Mediterranean Sea.

Page 71: Eisenach is an old city in the state of Thuringia in Germany. Wartburg, the famed castle where medieval minstrels competed in singing and Luther translated the Bible, and the house in which Bach was born are located in this region.

Page 72 : Esterházy, a palace in the Austrian capital of Vienna, contains a well-known restaurant and wine tavern in its cellars.

Glühwein is red wine with sugar, honey, and spices, heated warm.

"Heurige" usually denotes an Austrian wine tavern but can also (as in this poem) refer to new Austrian wine.

Page 73: On January 7, 2013, a euro was equivalent to $1.30.

Page 85: This poem refers to the Korean novelist Hong Seong-Won (1937 – 2008).

Page 86: Mi-Baek is the pen name of Korean novelist Yi Chong-Jun (1939 –2008).

Bad Honnef is a small resort city by the Rhine in the German state of North Rhine-Westphalia.

Page 91: This poem refers to Stephen Kim Sou-Whan (1922–2009), who was a Roman Catholic cardinal and former Archbishop of Seoul. He was much revered in his lifetime and much mourned after his death.

A Poetic Voice for the Weak

Kim Tae-Whan

Kim Kwang-Kyu's poems are dedicated to the weak. Who and what are the weak? They are the underpriviledged and the unnoticed who, by relinquishing themselves, enable others. The "stone wall of dry-stacked/ black-basalt" that "never falls" because of the "many small holes / in those rocks" ("House at Mulmoe") are approximations of them. One important message in this collection—though by no means the only one—is that the weak make this a better world in which to live. Kim sees contemporary culture as favoring the strong and pressuring us to be strong, too. Eventually the weak are silenced and forgotten.

Once the disjunction between the weak and the strong is established, we can easily make a list showing which is which. For example, "a small truck with loudspeaker blaring" clearly belongs to the strong. Noise "exceeding eighty decibels" from the loudspeaker "drills through our ears." What is the difference between a noise that arouses longing and a noise that bombards the listener's ears? Nominally, it's the difference between a human voice and an artificial voice from a loudspeaker; fundamentally, it is the difference between a weak voice and a strong voice. A cadre of vendors selling fish, albeit a rarity these days, called for buyers with small voices that didn't harrow listeners' ears. Theirs was not a mere cry of solicitation but a riff with melody and rhythm. They didn't raise their voices just to sell their things but went about singing to people, and their songs remained in the poet's memory as a part of the pleasure of their wares. Then what about the sound from the fishmonger's loudspeaker? The instant his truck shows up "the whole village is astir." At the same time, "over fences, through windows, / seafood / deluges every household." The loudspeaker raises a ruckus as it forces its way through windows and into one's ears, an inescapable noise heedless of one's wishes, ultimately leaving a fishlike smell of death, indelible even after its departure.

The noise from the loudspeaker dwindles away,
but the smell of fish spreads like an echo
lingers with us no matter how much we wash—

like the odor of our own slow deaths.
—from "When the Fishmonger Arrives"

Here the desire for self-display in the fastest, surest way, blindly intrudes into another's realm without any thought of truly touching another's mind. It seems that the blustering noise from loudspeakers drove away the sounds of the vendors and went on to conquer streets, markets, TV, then the whole world. Henceforth, nobody will pay attention or listen to you unless you have a strong, tough voice. How, then, shall we redeem weak voices? This is Kim's poetic task.

When you juxtapose stillness and noise, the weak are placed near stillness. The weak are almost voiceless in this noisy world. But they are not sunken in total silence. Through their own subtle gestures, they too let us know of their existence. A poet must be sufficiently aware to respond to the meager messages of the weak. In "Trumpet Vine," the poet is walking along an alley one summer afternoon. He hears "a guitar strumming / Happy Birthday" somewhere. The sound wasn't to be considered a "weak'"one as mentioned above, but an element which constitutes the tumult of the world, but we, however, note a feeble message amidst all this:

Something softly taps my head.
The outstretched, orange hand
of a trumpet vine creeping
up a jujube tree behind the fence
has turned to look at me.
It's like the innocent eye
of a child gazing at an adult..
—from "Trumpet Vine"

Kim doesn't see the trumpet vine as simply blossoming regardless of whether people notice it or not. It makes a gesture to the poet walking by, as if asking him to look at it. The focal point here is that it does not grab the poet and bid him look at it but softly taps his head as if too shy to speak. The adverb "softly" is particularly significant as softness is characteristic of the weak. The poet's response to this delicate gesture proves to be a boon. Upon lifting his head, he sees the orange blossoms as "the innocent eyes / of a child" and savors joyful rapport.

He refers to these subtle gestures made by the weak as "signs," and he senses them everywhere.

With my feet on the terrace stones,
I was tying my old shoe
when, with a soft snap,
a hand brushed against my back.
It was a magnolia signaling autumn
as its silver leaves, lush all summer long,
have faded and now fall.

—"Sign of Autumn"

The Korean dictionary defines "sign" as "a sound or an indication made with the intention to let the other know of one's presence." A sign is a manifestation of one's presence made to communicate and make one's presence known. The most decisive way to inform of one's presence is to say "I'm here!" So why do people sometimes make their presence known by some sign, such as gently clearing the throat? The intent is to approach another without disturbance or surprise. In other words, a sign is the very means by which the weak communicate. When Kim speaks of the "sign of autumn," the expression indicates that the tree is sending a message to inform him of its presence. That message is nevertheless indirect and symptomatic, so much so that one can barely perceive the hidden intention behind it. How in the world can there be any meaning in a faded leaf brushing one's back? Signs, which are messages from the weak, are easily overlooked or ignored, but Kim doesn't disregard such messages. In a faded leaf falling and brushing his back, he senses the tree touching him to communicate.

But sensing a sign doesn't end with the realization that there's a being there; it means that I finally recognize it as a being which is nudging me, talking to me, and therefore exists with me. The following poem portrays such an understanding:

Standing on her hind legs,
her front paws on the window frame,
Bokshil peers into the room and meets
my eyes. With no noise from inside,
she probably thought no one was home.

Bouyed by the coffee I had late in the afternoon,
I pore over writing I've long neglected
until, sensing someone's presence,
I turn and look outside.
There high in the night sky
the full moon peers into my window.
Everyone has gone.
I'm home by myself
but I'm not alone.

—"Home by Myself"

The reiteration of the phrase "peers into" in this poem establishes a correlation between the poet's dog and the full moon. Hence, we can take the whole poem as being crafted in a variant form, largely because it is composed of two parts. Lines one to seven comprise the first part; seven through fourteen the second.

Bokshil peers inside the room, not expecting to find anyone, but then her eyes unexpectedly meet those of the owner. The dog thought she was home alone, but in truth was not. The poet has a similar realization. He thought everyone had gone and he was mulling over his writing alone. Then he sees the full moon peering through the window and realizes he has company. The poet's own misunderstanding and ensuing realization were predicted in Bokshil's.

Instead of being a mere third object, the full moon proves to be a being coexistent with the poet and the dog. This is signified when he states that it began with a sign:

until sensing someone's presence,
I turn and look outside;

Reacting to the moon's subtle message, the poet is no longer alone. He's realized the presence of the moon, his companion.

Baek Nam-Jun once called the moon the oldest television in the world. The brightest full moon makes a very weak diversion in an age when a plethora of dazzling, moving images captures our attention. By receiving and deciphering an extremely feeble message from this old television, Kim Kwang-Kyu retreives it from a bog of oblivion and disregard. This is the very moment when the poetic task to redeem the weak is achieved.

However, this poses a question: Is the poet who deciphers these messages weak or strong?

> That evening when the lights and noise
> from a makeshift stage in the public square
> assaulted our ears and eyes,
> the old poet I ran across on lawn across from city hall
> offered me his ice-cold hand.
> Then dragging a body almost too feeble to walk,
> he receded slowly into the dark distance.
> I reemembered a book purchased five decades ago:
> a collection of his poems, its covers tattered.
> I wish I'd asked him to sign the book.
> An autumn butterfly barely managed to fly away,
> appearing about to drop and alight on the ground
> like a leaf falling in the chill of a late autumn night.
>
> —"Autumn Butterfly"

It is not hard to find a marked contrast between the strong and the weak. On one hand are these brazen "lights and noise from a makeshift stage in the public square/ assaulted our eyes and ears," and on the other an old poet wearily hauling "a body almost too feeble to walk" and receding slowly "into the dark distance" and "a collection of his poems, its covers tattered." The frail old poet dwindles in the face of the blasting lights and jarring noise. Moreover, the message from the tattered collection of his poems is quite faint. In addition, the cold hand implies that the old poet is approaching death and nothingness. Despite all this, he is in the sight of a keen compassionate observer, and watching as the old poets disappears into the darkness, the observer produces a somber beautiful image of "an autumn butterfly that barely managed to fly away / appearing as if about to drop and alight on the ground / like a leaf falling in the chill of a late autumn night."

Significantly, the weak one whom Kim wishes to reclaim is a fellow poet, someone not so different from himself. This implies that while a poet may redeem another poet, a poem redeems itself. The identical nature of subject and object indicates that the poet resembling the "autumn butterfly" as described by Kim, and the image of the old "collection of poems" whose covers are in tatters may be projected at Kim himself. In other words, the poet in a way is talking about himself and projecting himself into the future. Therefore this poem can be construed as his own weak sound or sign.

But how can a poet redeem another poet if he, himself, is a weak being and his poem his subtle sign of himself? Will he not fall into the bog himself while attempting to get them out of that pit of oblivion and disregard? What if the blustering loudspeaker drowns him out? Shouldn't a poem which aims to redeem the weak deliver a message that can overcome a forklift's power or lighting's glare?

Kim doesn't consider it redemption to uncover something that has been forgotten and then present it to this turbulent world. Being ignored, forgotten and buried are the marks of the weak and these things help to make them worthy, so a poet who writes about the weak being shouldn't be rash. It's here! I've found it! Please look at this! Never does the poet raise his voice this way. If a poem assumes a strong voice, it alters and destroys the weak one being portrayed in the poem.

Interspersed in this collection are obscure things, such as the "Airport Near the Beach." It's not a place people deliberately look for, but it does reveal itself in an unforeseen way at a chance moment.

> A quiet airport near the beach.
> A small jet leaves for Paris four times a day.
> Its silver wings soar above the sea
> in the bright Mediterranean sun,
> through lavender-scented, crystal-clear air.
> The staff closes the customs office at eleven a.m.
> and steps out for lunch. A few foreigners
> who missed their flights
> have been lounging in the lobby,
> but they now walk to the restaurant on the second floor
> where they'll drink wine from Provence
> while waiting for the afternoon plane.
> They may remember this brief unscheduled rest
> longer than they'll remember a famous scenic spot.

—"Airport Near the Beach"

The airport near the beach is a transit place where travelers briefly stay on their way to their destinations. This place is not a tourist attraction like Niagara Falls, which pulls those who do not "mind tedious long-distance flights and packing troublesome luggage." If Niagara Falls can be called a strong place, the airport by the beach in the town of Toulon is a weak place. Foreign travelers—the poet can be presumed to be among them—are detained here for a fairly long time, due to unforeseen circumstances. Yet this is a fortuitous event during a tight travel schedule, granting the poet a chance to breathe, and he opens his eyes to the beauty surrounding this small quiet airport. The travelers, he muses, will remember this place longer than some attractions they've visited.

Is Kim then trying to tout the airport in Toulon as a nice retreat where one can relish "the bright Mediterranean sun" and "wine from Provence?" No, but the unsophisticated atmosphere and the unexpected leisure fascinate him. It is a weak place, sequestered and therefore quite unnoticed, and his desire is not to illuminate what is concealed, but to steal into the hidden world and be a part of it, and thereby be happy in the fellowship. The impulse to get off at an unfamiliar countryside station and spend the rest of his life there alone stems from the same desire. Consequently, it's not the poet who redeems the weak, but the weak that redeem the poet.

The weak, in truth, are not altogether weak. Even if the strong and their noise appear to inundate and rule the earth, this world still subsists because of the hidden weak. High-rise apartment buildings don't hold the enormous city together. Rather, the poet seems to say, it is bound by "the mountain preserved like a small oasis / amidst Euju-ro, Morene-gil and Yunhhi-ro, / enclosed by high-rise apartments" ("A Native Squirrel"). And Mount Goeun, pent-up in the heart of a big city, is the perfect analogy for the message in Kim's poems: stillness barely perceivable amidst the noise. Yet, Kim tells us, we must be able to hear this stillness, for it constitutes our redemption.

THE POET

Kim Kwang-Kyu was born in Seoul in 1941. He received his undergraduate and graduate degrees in German Literature at Seoul National University and later studied in Munich, Germany. He debuted as a poet in 1975 with *Literature and Intellect,* a quarterly magazine. He received the Nokwon Literature Award in 1979 for *Steeped in Our Last Dream,* the first collection of his poems; the Kim Su-Young Literature Award in 1983 for *No, It Isn't So,* his second collection; the Pyonwoon Literature Award for *Ahniri,* his fifth collection; the Daesan Literature Award in 2003 for *When We First Met,* his eighth collection; and recently the Eesan Literature Award for *Soft Hand of Time,* his ninth collection. His other poetry books are *The Heart of the Great Mountain, Like a Good-for-Nothing, Waterways, Though I Have Nothing, Faint Shadows of Love,* and *For Someone.* His prose works include *Natural Voice and Falsetto* and *Stairway You Slowly Ascend,* and his academic research work includes *On Guinnter Ahheehi.* His translations into Korean from German include Bertolt Brecht's *The Survivor's Sorrow,* and Heinrich Heine's *Lorelei,* as well as *Die Tiefe der Muschel* and *Botchaften vom grünen Pleneten. Faint Shadows of Love* and *The Depths of a Clam* have been translated into English, and a Chinese translation of *Faint Shadows of Love* was published subsequently. He received the Friedrich Gundolf Cultural Merit Award from the German Academy for Language and Literature (2006) and the Yee Mi-Reuk Award from the Korean German Association (2008). He is Professor Emeritus of German literature at Hanyang University.

THE TRANSLATOR

Cho Young-Shil, a retired English teacher, now works as a poet and translator. Her previous translations include Anna Seon's *You, Me, Us* and Choi Min-Kyung's *Life with My Departed Grandmother.* Her translation of *Loving Promises* by Helen S. Rice was published in Korea by Voice Publishers in 1988. Poems for young adults written by Ms. Cho have appeared in various literary magazines in Korea since her debut in 2007. She has received grants from the Korea Literature Translation Institute for the English translations of *You, Me, Us,* Kwon Young-Poom's *A Cat Who Lost His Tail, Life with My Departed Grandmother,* and Kim Kwang-Kyu's *One Day, Then Another.*

The Korean Voices Series

One Day, Then Another: Poems by Kim Kwang-Kyu
Translated by Cho Young-Shil
Volume 18 978-1-935210-54-2 104 pages $16.00

Magnolia & Lotus: Selected Poems of Hyesim
Translated by Ian Haight and T'ae-yong Ho
Volume 17 978-1-935210-43-6 96 pages $16.00

This Side of Time: Selected Poems by Ko Un
Translated by Claire You and Richard Silberg
Volume 16 978-1-935210-32-0 100 pages $16.00

Borderland Roads: Selected Poems of Ho Kyun
Translated by Ian Haight and T'ae-yong Ho
Volume 15 978-1-935210-08-5 102pages $16.00

Scale and Stairs: Selected Poems of Heeduk Ra
Translated by Won-chung Kim and Christopher Merrill
Volume 14 978-1-893996-24-3 88 pages $17.00

One Human Family & Other Stories - Stories by Chung Yeun-hee
Translated by Hyun-jae Yee Sallee
Volume 13 978-1-893996-87-8 232 pages $16.00

Woman on the Terrace - Poems by Moon Chung-hee
Translated by Seong-kon Kim and Alec Gordon
Volume 12 978-1-87399686-1 120 pages $18.00

Eyes of Dew - Poems by Chonggi Mah
Translated by Brother Anthony of Taizé
Volume 11 1-893996-79-4$ 160 pages 16.00

Even Birds Leave the World: Selected Poems of Ji-woo Hwang
Translated by Won-chun Kim & Christopher Merrill
Volume 10 1-893996-45-x 104 pages $14.00

The Depths of a Clam: Selected Poems of Kim Kwang-kyu
Translated by Brother Anthony of Taize
Volume 9 1-893996-43-3 160 pages $16.00

Echoing Song: Contemporary Korean Women Poets
Edited by Peter H. Lee
Volume 8 1-893996-35-2 304 pages $18.00

Among the Flowering Reeds: Classic Korean Poems in Chinese
Edited and translated by Kim Jong-gil
Volume 7 1-893996-54-9 152 pages $16.00

Brother Enemy: Poems of the Korean War
Edited and translated by Suh Ji-moon
Volume 6 1-893996-20-4 176 pages $16.00

Shrapnel and Other Stories - Stories of Dong-ha Lee
Translated by Hyun-jae Yee Sallee
Volume 5 1-893996-53-0 176 pages $16.00

Strong Wind At Mishi Pass - Poems by Tong-gyu Hwang
Translated by Seong-kon Kim & Dennis Maloney
Volume 4 1-893996-10-7 118 pages $15.00

A Sketch of the Fading Sun - Stories of Wan-suh Park
Translated by Hyun-jae Yee Sallee
Volume 3 1-877727-93-8 200 pages $15.00

Heart's Agony: Selected Poems of Chiha Kim
Translated by Won-chun Kim and James Han
Volume 2 1-877727-84-9 128 pages $14.00 paper

The Snowy Road: An Anthology of Korean Fiction
Translated by Hyun-jae Yee Sallee
Volume 1 1-877727-19-9 168 pages $12.00 paper